denver

This hill is far
enough.
It's true. Either
you are here

or you're not. And
if you
are, this is the
place to stand . . .

CID CORMAN

denver

A PHOTOGRAPHIC SURVEY OF THE METROPOLITAN AREA

by Robert Adams

Colorado Associated University Press
in cooperation with
The State Historical Society of Colorado

I am grateful to the John Simon Guggenheim Memorial Foundation for a fellowship that enabled me to take the pictures, and to the National Endowment for the Arts, a federal agency, for a grant that made possible the publication of the book.

Cid Corman generously gave permission to quote from his poem "The Obbligato," taken from In Good Time *(copyright Cid Corman, 1964).*

Finally, I would like to note that interior and exterior scenes on adjoining pages are not necessarily of the same subject.

In Denver's vacant lots one can still find, no matter how numerous the food wrappers and pieces of styrofoam, an old, tough green — Spanish bayonet, cactus, and sage. Perhaps most reassuring of all, there remain cottonwoods, those commercially useless trees that are habitat for birds and children.

Whether I was photographing these accidental sanctuaries, however, or bare, new tracts, I tried to keep in mind a phrase from a novel by Kawabata: "My life, a fragment of a landscape." The same applied, I thought, to each of us, and to the objects with which we live. My goal was not only to record the animate and inanimate fragments, but to show the totality, the landscape.

Denver was, in the early part of the last decade, different in appearance from Los Angeles. In 1962, when I came home after several years in Southern California, I tried to photograph the city and the high altitude brilliance that distinguished it. New building had, it is true, begun to change some of the geography, but the light was clean enough to disinfect car agencies and cheap bungalows; smog was so rare, in fact, that I refused to photograph when it was present. Bad light was just not typical.

By the end of the decade it was. A new city had emerged (though one that looked prematurely worn), a city much like other large urban centers across the Southwest. To show it accurately required that I stop sorting things out by the degree to which they were picturesque; if beauty were to be discovered in Denver, it had to be on the basis of a radical faith in inclusion. Shopping centers, junky arroyos, and commercial streets not only had to be more fully acknowledged, but acknowledged amidst the dull, hard gray of pollution.

I determined, moreover, to stay clear of the mountains. I distrusted the late Victorians' passion for mountaintop vistas, and decided instead to adopt the perspective of the first settlers, those who saw Colorado from the small rises of the prairie.

The subject of these pictures is, then, a troubling mixture: buildings and roads that are often, but not always, unworthy of us; people who are, though they participate in urban chaos, admirable and deserving of our thought and care; light that sometimes still works an alchemy; a western scale that, despite our crowding, persists in long views.

If I hope the pictures show more than this, it is because I share the goal of most photographers. You may have sensed what that goal is if you have watched someone with a camera struggle for adequate results; over and over again he walks a few steps and peers, rather comically, into the camera; to the exasperation of family and friends, he inventories what seems an endless number of angles; he explains, if asked, that he is trying for effective composition, but hesitates to define it. Edward Weston, a photographer who demonstrated he knew what it was, said simply that good composition was "the strongest way of seeing." What he appears to have meant was that a photographer wants Form, an unarguably right relationship of shapes, a visual stability in which all components are equally important. The photographer hopes, in brief, to discover a tension so exact that it is peace.

Pictures that embody this calm are not synonymous, of course, with what we might see casually out a car window (they may, however, be more effective if we can be tricked into thinking so). The form the photographer records, though discovered in a split second of literal fact, is different because it implies an order beyond itself, a landscape into which all fragments, no matter how imperfect, fit perfectly.

Land Surrounded; To Be Developed

11

21

Factories; Industrial Land

33

Our Homes

41

63

69

73

Trees

77

Shopping Centers; Commercial Land

Roads

Agricultural Land in the Path of Development

111

CAPTIONS